Google Pixel Watch 3
User Guide

Customizing your Device
Experience

Linda B. Jordan

Copyright

Table of Contents

1. Unboxing and Initial Setup
Included in the box:
Google Pixel Watch 3 (41mm or 45mm)
Charging cable and magnetic charging dock
Quick start guide
Initial Setup:
1. Charge Your Watch: Place the watch on the charging dock to charge it fully.
2. Download the Pixel Watch App:
On your phone, download the Pixel Watch app from the Google Play Store (Android) or App Store (iOS).
The app will guide you through pairing the watch with your phone.
3. Sign In to Google Account: Follow the on-screen prompts to sign in with your Google account.
4. Pairing: Once signed in, the app will search for your Pixel Watch. Select it and pair.

2. Navigating the Watch
Buttons:
Rotating Crown (Home Button): Rotate to scroll through menus and apps. Press to return to the home screen or to open the app list.

Flat Button: Located beneath the crown. It opens your recent apps. You can also double-press it to open Google Pay or press and hold to activate Google Assistant.

Display:

Touchscreen Interface: Swipe to navigate the watch face, apps, and settings.

Always-On Display: The watch has an always-on option, which shows the time and basic info when not actively in use.

Brightness Adjustment: Swipe down from the top of the screen and adjust the brightness if needed.

3. Watch Faces and Customization

Changing Watch Faces:

1. Open the Pixel Watch app on your phone.

2. Go to Watch Faces and choose from available options or download new faces from the Google Play Store.

3. Tap Apply to set your preferred face.

Customization:

Complications: You can add or remove complications (widgets) to show useful information like heart rate, weather, steps, etc.

Settings > Personalize allows further customization of the watch face appearance, complications, and other display features.

4. Fitness and Health Tracking

Fitness Tracking:

1. The Pixel Watch 3 supports various fitness activities like walking, running, cycling, and swimming (IP68 water resistance).

2. Automatic Workout Detection: It will detect workouts like walking or running after a few minutes and log them automatically.

3. Use the Fitbit integration for detailed analysis of workouts, sleep, and more.

Heart Rate and Health Sensors:

Track continuous heart rate and get ECG readings via the Fitbit app.

Blood Oxygen (SpO2) tracking is available overnight or through specific settings in the health app.

Skin Temperature and Conductance are also tracked for a full picture of your well-being.

Special Features:

Emergency Detection: If the watch detects a lack of pulse (due to serious health events), it will automatically alert emergency services.

Sleep Tracking: Syncs with the Fitbit app to track sleep patterns, including the readiness score to assess your recovery and readiness for exercise.

5. Notifications and Connectivity

Notifications:

Receive notifications for calls, texts, emails, and apps.

Notifications from your phone will appear on your Pixel Watch as standalone messages (not bundled).

You can interact with notifications, such as replying to messages via voice or preset replies.

Connectivity:

Bluetooth: Ensure Bluetooth is turned on for syncing with your phone.

Wi-Fi 6 and LTE (Optional): If your model supports LTE, you can use the watch independently without your phone for calls, texts, and data.
NFC: For payments through Google Pay.
UWB (Ultra-Wideband): Works with compatible Pixel phones for unlocking features.

6. Managing Apps and Features
Downloading Apps:
1. Open the Google Play Store on your watch or phone.
2. Browse or search for apps designed for Wear OS and install them directly to your watch.
Health and Fitness Apps:
Use Fitbit for detailed workout, health, and sleep data.
Additional third-party apps can be installed for specific workouts, like running or yoga.
Google Assistant:
Use the Google Assistant for voice commands, such as setting reminders, controlling smart home devices, or answering questions.
Music and Media:
Sync music from Spotify, YouTube Music, or other services.
Control music playback directly from your watch when paired with Bluetooth headphones.

7. Battery and Charging
Battery Life:
The 41mm model lasts up to 24 hours on a full charge, while the 45mm model lasts up to 36 hours.
Battery Saver Mode: Extend battery life by limiting non-essential functions like heart rate tracking.

Charging:

Place your watch on the magnetic charging dock for a full charge (typically takes around 1-2 hours).

The watch supports fast charging, so you can quickly top up if needed.

8. Troubleshooting and Maintenance

Software Updates:

Regular updates will be pushed through the Pixel Watch app. Make sure your watch is connected to Wi-Fi and sufficiently charged to complete updates.

Resetting the Watch:

If you encounter issues, you can perform a factory reset by going to Settings > System > Reset. This will erase all data from your watch, so be sure to back up important information first.

Handling Fragility:

The curved glass dome is susceptible to scratches or cracks. Consider using a screen protector or case.

If damaged, your only option is to replace the watch as there are no repair services available for the Pixel Watch 3.

9. Additional Features and Tips

Wear OS Features:

Google Pay for contactless payments (set up through the app).

Google Assistant for voice control of various functions.

Fitness Challenges can be set up via the Fitbit app.

Access smart home devices with the Google Home app.

Chapter 1.

Unboxing and Initial Setup Included in the box:

When you first receive your Google Pixel Watch 3, the excitement of unboxing and setting up your new smartwatch can be thrilling. This section provides a detailed guide on the unboxing process, the items included in the box, and step-by-step instructions for the initial setup. Whether you're upgrading from an older model or venturing into the world of smartwatches for the first time, getting started is easy with the following instructions.

Included in the Box:

Opening the box for the Google Pixel Watch 3 reveals a sleek, high-quality package designed to protect your watch and its accessories during shipping. Here's what you will find inside:

1. Google Pixel Watch 3 (41mm or 45mm):

The main event. Your new smartwatch comes in two size options, 41mm and 45mm, allowing you to choose the perfect fit for your wrist. The watch features a premium circular AMOLED display that provides vibrant colors and sharp resolution, making it not only functional but stylish as well. It's lightweight and features an all-glass dome with a polished stainless steel body, giving it an elegant appearance while remaining robust enough for daily wear. Whether you're at work or at the gym, the Pixel Watch 3 is designed to suit any environment with ease.

2. Charging Cable and Magnetic Charging Dock:

Alongside the Pixel Watch 3, you'll find a charging cable and a magnetic charging dock. The charging dock features a convenient magnetic system that allows the watch to snap into place easily for charging. This docking system ensures that the watch remains securely in position while charging, preventing accidental disconnections. The cable length is designed to be long enough to provide flexibility in where you set your watch while it charges, ensuring that you won't have to move things around just to connect your new smartwatch.

3. Quick Start Guide:

If you're new to wearables or the Pixel Watch, the included Quick Start Guide is your first point of reference. The guide provides a simple, visual step-by-step process for setting up your watch, with instructions on charging it, downloading the necessary apps, and pairing with your phone. It's a great starting point to understand the basics of getting your watch up and running.

Initial Setup:

Now that you have unboxed your Google Pixel Watch 3, it's time to set it up and begin using it. The setup process is simple, taking only a few minutes if you follow the steps outlined below.

Step 1: Charge Your Watch

Before diving into any setup process, it's important to ensure your Pixel Watch 3 has enough charge to complete the setup. Even though the watch may come partially charged out of the box, it's recommended to charge it fully to prevent any interruptions during setup.

To charge your Pixel Watch 3:

1. Place the watch on the magnetic charging dock:

The charging dock has a built-in magnetic system that securely holds the watch in place. Make sure the watch's charging pins align with the dock's charging contacts. The magnetic feature helps ensure a stable connection between the watch and the charger, allowing for efficient charging.

2. Connect the charging cable to a power source:

Plug the other end of the charging cable into a USB port on your computer, a wall adapter, or a power bank. The charging dock should show a small indicator light or display a charging icon on your watch screen to confirm the watch is charging properly.

While the charging process begins, this is a good time to get your phone ready for pairing. The initial setup process can take anywhere between 30 minutes to an hour, depending on your internet speed and the updates your watch may need.

Step 2: Download the Pixel Watch App

The next step in setting up your Google Pixel Watch 3 is to download the Pixel Watch app on your smartphone. The app is necessary to pair your phone with the watch and to manage various settings and features on the device.

1. Open the Google Play Store (for Android) or the App Store (for iOS):

Search for the Pixel Watch app.

2. Download the App:

Once located, tap on the Download or Install button to begin the download process. The app is free and works on both Android and iOS devices, although some features may be exclusive to Android.

Once the app is installed on your phone, open it. You will be greeted with a prompt to sign in using your Google account. This is where you link the watch to your Google ecosystem,

13

allowing you to sync data across devices, including Google Fit, Gmail, and other Google services.

Step 3: Sign In to Google Account

In this step, you'll be prompted to sign in to your Google account. If you already have a Google account, enter your credentials. If not, you can quickly create one by selecting the option to sign up for a new account.

Signing in to your Google account is crucial as it enables you to use Google services directly on your Pixel Watch, such as syncing data, using Google Assistant, and receiving notifications from apps connected to your Google account. Additionally, when paired with a Google Pixel phone, your Pixel Watch 3 will integrate more seamlessly with your phone's ecosystem.

Once signed in, your phone will automatically begin searching for nearby Pixel Watch devices.

Step 4: Pairing Your Watch

At this point, the Pixel Watch app will scan for available devices to pair with your phone. This process may take a few moments as the app searches for Bluetooth signals emitted by the watch.

1. Select your watch model:

Once the watch appears on the screen, select it. The app will show you a confirmation message that the watch is being connected to your phone.

2. Confirm the Pairing:

You may be prompted to confirm the pairing on both the watch and the phone. This ensures that the connection is secure and that you're pairing the correct device.

Once paired, your Google Pixel Watch 3 will begin syncing with your phone, and the setup process will proceed with updates, setting preferences, and downloading any necessary apps or system updates. This may take a few more minutes, but once completed, your watch is ready to use.

With the watch set up and paired, you can start customizing it, exploring the watch faces, and taking advantage of all the features Google has packed into the Pixel Watch 3. Whether you're using it for fitness tracking, notifications, or simply to tell the time, your watch will be ready to enhance your day-to-day life.

Chapter 2.

Navigating the Watch Buttons:

Navigating your Google Pixel Watch 3 is an intuitive process, thanks to its sleek design and user-friendly interface. Whether you're using physical buttons or the touchscreen, each navigation method is designed to enhance the overall experience, ensuring you can quickly access the features you need. In this chapter, we'll walk you through the primary ways to interact with your watch: the Rotating Crown, Flat Button, and Display features.

Buttons:

The Google Pixel Watch 3 has two main physical buttons that serve a variety of functions. These buttons are located on the side of the watch for easy access while you're wearing it, and each button provides distinct navigation options.

1. Rotating Crown (Home Button):

The Rotating Crown is the most important physical control on the Google Pixel Watch 3, serving both as a scroll wheel and a button. Located at the side of the watch, this crown can be rotated and pressed, each action serving a different purpose.

Rotating the Crown:

When you rotate the crown, it allows you to scroll through different menus and apps on the watch. This makes navigation smooth and fluid, especially when browsing through long lists or settings options. The tactile feel of the crown as it turns offers satisfying feedback, making it easy to track your movement through menus.

Pressing the Crown:

Pressing the rotating crown has two main functions:

Return to Home Screen:

A single press of the crown brings you back to the watch's home screen, regardless of where you are in the watch's interface. This is a quick way to exit out of any app or screen and return to the main display.

Open App List:

When you press and hold the crown, it opens the app list, showing you all the apps installed on the watch. This allows you to switch between apps without having to swipe through multiple screens.

The Rotating Crown is a highly functional tool that offers both ease of access and fine control over the watch's interface, making it a key element of the Pixel Watch 3's design.

2. Flat Button:

The Flat Button is located just below the rotating crown and serves as a secondary control for the Pixel Watch 3. While it is slightly smaller than the crown, it is no less important in navigating your smartwatch experience.

Recent Apps:

A single press of the Flat Button will show you your recently opened apps. This makes it easy to quickly switch between apps, whether you're checking notifications, tracking a workout, or accessing settings.

Google Pay (Double-Press):

For users who have set up Google Pay on their Pixel Watch 3, double-pressing the Flat Button will open Google Pay. From there, you can make contactless payments simply by holding your watch near a compatible terminal. This feature is especially convenient when you're on the go and need to make a payment without pulling out your phone or wallet.

Google Assistant (Press and Hold):

Pressing and holding the Flat Button activates Google Assistant, allowing you to interact with the watch using your voice. You can ask Google Assistant questions, set reminders, control smart home devices, check the weather, or even send messages all without needing to touch the screen.

These two buttons Rotating Crown and Flat Button work together to make your experience with the Pixel Watch 3 seamless and efficient. Each button has a distinct role that enhances the ease of use, and their combination allows for smooth multitasking between different features and apps.

Display:

The Display of the Google Pixel Watch 3 is a key element that provides you with rich, detailed information while allowing for easy interaction via touch. The watch's high-resolution AMOLED display not only offers vibrant colors but also ensures that everything on the screen is sharp and clear, whether it's your watch face or app icons. Below are some of the key aspects of the display you should know about to get the most out of your watch:

1. Touchscreen Interface:

The Pixel Watch 3 features a highly responsive touchscreen interface, which is the main method of interaction when navigating through apps and settings.

Swiping:

Swiping is the primary gesture to navigate around the watch. You can swipe left, right, up, or down depending on the context. Swiping from the top of the screen brings up the quick settings menu, where you can adjust various features like brightness, Wi-Fi, Do Not Disturb, and more. Swiping from the bottom of the screen brings up your notifications, allowing you to quickly view and dismiss alerts. Swiping from left to right will often help you go back to previous screens, and right to left might show additional options or panels within apps.

Tapping:

To open apps, view detailed information, or select options in menus, a simple tap on the touchscreen is all that's required. Tapping is intuitive and works similarly to tapping on any other touchscreen device, making it feel familiar and easy to navigate.

Long Pressing:

Long pressing the screen can open up more options in certain apps, such as setting or customizing watch faces, or opening widgets. It's a great way to quickly make changes or check additional information.

The responsive nature of the Pixel Watch's touchscreen allows for smooth navigation, and the combination of touch gestures and physical buttons creates a fluid experience.

2. Always-On Display:

One of the standout features of the Google Pixel Watch 3 is its Always-On Display (AOD), which allows you to glance at the time and essential information without needing to wake up the watch. This feature is particularly useful when you need to check the time quickly or view health stats like heart rate, steps, or notifications while the watch is in idle mode.

The Always-On Display uses a low-power mode to preserve battery life while still displaying crucial information. You can customize the content of the AOD to show different complications, such as the time, date, weather, or fitness data. This means that, even when the watch is not actively in use, you'll always have access to important details at a glance.

Activating or Deactivating the AOD:

To toggle the Always-On Display feature, swipe down from the top of the screen, and you can find the AOD settings within the quick settings menu. Enabling or disabling this option is a matter of tapping the AOD icon to toggle between the two modes.

3. Brightness Adjustment:

Sometimes, you may need to adjust the brightness of your Pixel Watch 3's display, especially when using the watch in bright environments like outdoors or in low-light conditions at night.

Adjusting Brightness:

To adjust the brightness, simply swipe down from the top of the screen. This opens the quick settings menu, where you'll see the brightness slider. You can then swipe left or right to decrease or increase the brightness, depending on your environment. This gives you easy control over how bright your display is without having to navigate deep into settings.

Auto-Brightness:

Alternatively, you can enable Auto-Brightness, which automatically adjusts the display's brightness based on ambient light. This feature helps conserve battery life, as the screen won't be as bright in darker environments. It's a smart way to balance usability and battery conservation throughout the day.

Conclusion:

The navigation system on the Google Pixel Watch 3 combines intuitive gestures with practical physical buttons, creating a streamlined experience that's easy to learn and use. Whether you're rotating the crown, tapping on the touchscreen, or adjusting settings, the watch allows you to effortlessly interact with its many features. From making payments with a double press of the flat button to adjusting brightness for outdoor use, the Google Pixel Watch 3 is built for simplicity and efficiency, making it a perfect companion for everyday life.

Chapter 3.

Watch Faces and Customization

One of the most appealing features of the Google Pixel Watch 3 is the ability to fully customize the watch face. Watch faces are not just about aesthetics; they serve as the central hub for viewing important information and making the most out of the watch's capabilities. Whether you want a simple, classic look or a more detailed display with widgets and data, the Pixel Watch 3 offers a wide range of options to match your style and needs. This chapter will walk you through the process of changing watch faces and customizing them to suit your preferences.

Changing Watch Faces:

The first step in personalizing your Pixel Watch 3 is choosing a watch face that reflects your style. Google offers a variety of watch faces, each designed to provide different aesthetics and functionalities. Some are simple and elegant, while others display detailed information such as fitness stats, weather updates, or calendar events. Here's how you can change the watch face:

1. Open the Pixel Watch App on Your Phone:

To begin customizing your watch face, you need to access the Pixel Watch app on your smartphone. This app serves as the central control hub for managing all settings on your watch. If you haven't already installed it, you can download the app from the Google Play Store (for Android) or the App Store (for iOS).

2. Browse Available Watch Faces:

Once the app is installed and connected to your Pixel Watch 3, tap on the Watch Faces option. This section of the app offers a variety of preloaded watch faces that you can choose from. You can scroll through the list of options and preview how each watch face looks on your device. The app provides both minimalistic designs and more data-packed layouts to suit your lifestyle.

3. Download New Watch Faces from the Google Play Store:

If you want to expand your options, you can also browse and download additional watch faces from the Google Play Store. To do this, look for the "More Watch Faces" button in the Pixel Watch app, which will redirect you to the Play Store section specifically designed for wearable watch faces. There are plenty of options available, ranging from digital displays to analog-style faces, as well as highly customizable designs that let you integrate third-party complications like fitness tracking widgets, calendars, and more.

4. Apply Your Preferred Watch Face:

After you've browsed the available options and found one you like, simply tap on it to select it. The app will allow you to apply the selected face to your watch instantly. The new watch face will be synchronized with your Pixel Watch 3 and displayed on your wrist. If you're using a larger 45mm model, you'll find that the watch face automatically adjusts to the size of your screen, ensuring an optimal fit. You can always revisit the app later to change the face whenever you like.

Customizing the Watch Face:

Changing the watch face is only the beginning of the customization process. The Pixel Watch 3 allows you to go even further by personalizing the appearance and functionality of the watch face using various settings. Here's how you can tailor the watch face to display information that's most important to you:

1. Complications:

Complications are small widgets or indicators on your watch face that display additional information. Depending on the watch face you've selected, you may be able to add or remove complications to show data such as heart rate, steps, battery status, calendar events, weather forecasts, or even news updates. These allow you to get the most out of your watch by turning it into a fully functional tool for your daily life.

To add or remove complications:

Go to Settings > Personalize > Watch Face.

From there, you can tap on Complications and select from the available options.

Depending on the watch face, you may have different positions to place complications. For example, you might be able to add one complication at the top, one at the bottom, and another on the side.

The Pixel Watch 3 supports a range of complications from Google's own apps, including Google Fit for fitness data and Google Calendar for appointments. Additionally, third-party developers are creating new complications all the time, which you can install via the Play Store.

2. Personalizing the Watch Face Appearance:

The Settings > Personalize menu lets you adjust various aesthetic elements of your watch face. Here, you can alter elements like the color scheme, font styles, and the layout of complications. For example, you can switch from a light to a dark theme to suit your environment or personal preference. Dark themes are especially useful for saving battery life since they reduce the power consumption of OLED screens, like the one used on the Pixel Watch 3.

Adjusting Font and Size: Some watch faces allow you to change the font style or size, so you can make the text more readable or give it a more artistic flair. Choose from a range of fonts that suit the theme of your watch.

Changing the Color:

Many watch faces come with multiple color options. You can choose a color scheme that complements your outfit or matches the color of your watch band. Whether you prefer bold colors or subtle, muted tones, the customization options are extensive.

3. Additional Display Features:

In addition to changing the overall look and adding complications, the Pixel Watch 3 offers further options for adjusting your display. You can modify settings related to the always-on display, which shows basic time and information when the screen is inactive, ensuring you always have access to key data at a glance.

The always-on display can be customized to show only the time or include additional information such as the current date, weather, or heart rate. You can adjust the brightness to ensure the display is readable in all lighting conditions. Swipe down from the top of the screen, and you'll find a slider to adjust brightness or enable auto-brightness for optimal screen visibility.

<u>Tips for Efficient Customization:</u>

Keep It Simple:

While it's tempting to load up your watch face with as many complications as possible, too much information can make the display feel cluttered. Consider keeping the watch face clean and minimal by displaying only the most important data.

Experiment with Layouts:

Don't hesitate to try different combinations of watch faces and complications. Some faces may look better with certain complications, while others may offer a cleaner and more intuitive interface.

Consider Your Usage:

If you're into fitness, choose a watch face with prominent fitness tracking data. For busy professionals, a watch face that shows calendar events, emails, or notifications might be more useful.

By understanding the various customization options available on the Pixel Watch 3, you can make your device not just an accessory but a personalized extension of yourself. Whether it's adjusting the visual style, adding complications for easy access to information, or setting up a layout that suits your routine, the Pixel Watch 3 ensures that you have complete control over how your watch looks and functions.

Chapter 4.

Fitness and Health Tracking Fitness Tracking:

The Pixel Watch 3 is designed to help you take control of your health and fitness journey. With a variety of built-in sensors and features, it serves as more than just a timepiece it's an all-in-one fitness and health tracker that can monitor your daily activity, heart rate, sleep patterns, and even provide emergency alerts in case of serious health events. Whether you're a casual walker or a seasoned athlete, the Pixel Watch 3 provides the tools you need to stay on top of your fitness goals.

Fitness Tracking:

The Pixel Watch 3 supports an array of fitness activities, making it an ideal choice for individuals who enjoy a wide variety of physical activities. The watch is equipped to track both common and specialized exercises, with the ability to automatically detect when you're engaging in an activity.

1. Supported Fitness Activities:

The Pixel Watch 3 is versatile in its ability to track multiple fitness activities, including:

Walking:

Whether you're strolling around the block or on a long hike, the watch will track your steps, distance, and calories burned.

Running:

The watch captures running data such as pace, distance, and time. It can also provide feedback on your performance, helping you track improvements over time.

Cycling:

If you prefer cycling, the Pixel Watch 3 will monitor your route, speed, and duration, and even offer data on how many calories you burned.

Swimming:

With an IP68 water resistance rating, the Pixel Watch 3 is swim-proof and tracks your swim sessions. It records metrics like laps, stroke type, and the duration of your swim, all without worrying about water damage.

By supporting these and other activities, the Pixel Watch 3 allows you to track virtually any workout, making it an excellent companion for diverse fitness routines.

2. Automatic Workout Detection:

One of the key features of the Pixel Watch 3 is its automatic workout detection. The watch can recognize common workouts such as walking or running, even if you forget to manually start the tracking. It detects your movements after a few minutes and begins logging your workout automatically. This makes it easy for you to get credit for all your activity, even if you don't remember to start the timer.

This automatic feature is incredibly convenient, especially for people who don't want to interrupt their flow or lose track of their activity. You can view your workout data once the session is complete, and the watch will even suggest tracking a specific workout type based on your movements. When you stop the activity, the watch automatically stops recording, and the data is saved for later review.

3. Fitbit Integration:

The Fitbit integration with the Pixel Watch 3 enhances the watch's fitness tracking capabilities. After syncing your Pixel Watch 3 with the Fitbit app, you'll have access to an even more detailed analysis of your workouts, steps, and heart rate. The Fitbit app provides a holistic view of your fitness data, and you can review not only activity data but also insights into your sleep, exercise intensity, and long-term fitness progress.

Fitbit's Premium service takes this a step further by offering personalized fitness insights, guided workouts, and wellness reports that are tailored to your activity level. This integration gives you a comprehensive tool to track and improve your fitness journey, helping you set goals, monitor progress, and stay motivated.

Heart Rate and Health Sensors:

In addition to tracking activity, the Pixel Watch 3 is equipped with advanced health sensors that allow you to monitor vital signs like heart rate and blood oxygen levels. These sensors provide deeper insights into your overall well-being, ensuring that you're not just tracking your physical activity, but also keeping tabs on your body's internal health.

1. Continuous Heart Rate Monitoring:

The Pixel Watch 3 features continuous heart rate monitoring, which provides real-time data on how your heart is responding to physical activity. The watch tracks your heart rate throughout the day, even during periods of rest, to provide a baseline of your cardiovascular health.

During workouts, the watch records your heart rate in real time, allowing you to monitor how hard your body is working. It uses photoplethysmography (PPG) technology to measure blood flow and calculate your heart rate, offering accurate data for exercise performance and recovery. Whether you're running a marathon or walking to work, the Pixel Watch 3 ensures that you have an accurate record of how your heart rate fluctuates.

The data syncs with the Fitbit app, where you can monitor trends over time, including resting heart rate, exercise heart rate, and overall heart rate variability. These insights are valuable for assessing cardiovascular health and improving performance.

2. ECG Readings:

For those concerned about their heart health, the Pixel Watch 3 also includes the ability to take ECG (electrocardiogram) readings. An ECG measures the electrical activity of your heart and can help detect irregularities in heart rhythm, such as atrial fibrillation (AFib).

To take an ECG, you simply need to place your finger on the watch's crown and follow the instructions on the screen. The results are available in the Fitbit app, where they can be reviewed and saved for future reference. If the watch detects any unusual heart rhythms, it will alert you, allowing you to take prompt action. Regular ECG monitoring provides valuable insights into heart health, especially for people with a family history of heart conditions.

3. Blood Oxygen (SpO2) Tracking:

The Pixel Watch 3 tracks your blood oxygen (SpO2) levels, which is an important indicator of your overall health. SpO2 levels represent the amount of oxygen in your blood, and a drop in these levels can signify respiratory issues or other health concerns.

SpO2 tracking is available overnight, allowing you to monitor your levels while you sleep. Alternatively, you can activate it manually through the health app to track your levels during the day. This feature is especially useful for athletes or individuals who experience respiratory symptoms, as it provides a quick snapshot of how well your body is oxygenating blood during activity or rest.

4. Skin Temperature and Conductance:

The Pixel Watch 3 also features skin temperature and skin conductance sensors, which add further depth to your health tracking. Skin temperature readings offer insights into changes in your body temperature, which could indicate stress, illness, or other health conditions. Skin conductance, on the other hand, measures the moisture levels in your skin, which can reflect how your body is responding to stress, exercise, or emotional states.

By tracking both of these metrics, the Pixel Watch 3 helps you gain a better understanding of your physical state. These sensors are especially helpful for tracking changes in your body's reaction to stress, exercise, or environmental factors.

Special Features:

Beyond the standard fitness and health tracking features, the Pixel Watch 3 also includes special features that enhance its safety and functionality. These features are designed to provide additional peace of mind and ensure that your health is closely monitored at all times.

1. Emergency Detection:

In case of a health emergency, such as a serious fall or a lack of pulse, the Pixel Watch 3 can detect these events and automatically alert emergency services. This feature is especially valuable for individuals with medical conditions or those who exercise alone. If the watch detects a lack of heart rate, it will send an emergency alert with your location to ensure that help arrives quickly.

2. Sleep Tracking:

Sleep is a critical aspect of overall health, and the Pixel Watch 3 offers sleep tracking that syncs with the Fitbit app. The watch tracks the different stages of your sleep light, deep, and REM and provides a readiness score to assess how well-rested you are. The readiness score helps you determine if your body is recovered enough for the next day's activities.

By analyzing your sleep patterns, the Pixel Watch 3 provides insights into how your lifestyle and habits may be affecting your rest. Better sleep quality is linked to improved exercise performance, and the watch's sleep-tracking feature gives you the data needed to optimize your rest.

The Pixel Watch 3 is a powerhouse when it comes to fitness and health tracking. With its wide range of sensors, automatic workout detection, and integration with the Fitbit app, it provides comprehensive insights into your physical well-being. Whether you are tracking workouts, monitoring heart health, or seeking to improve your sleep, the Pixel Watch 3 is an essential companion on your journey to better fitness and overall health.

Chapter 5.

Notifications and Connectivity Notifications:

The Google Pixel Watch 3 bridges the gap between your smartphone and your daily life, delivering essential notifications and seamless connectivity options right on your wrist. Whether it's receiving calls, staying updated on important emails, or making payments on the go, the Pixel Watch 3 ensures you remain connected without constantly reaching for your phone. This chapter explores how the watch handles notifications and the advanced connectivity features that make it a powerful extension of your digital ecosystem.

Notifications:

Notifications on the Pixel Watch 3 are designed to keep you informed and responsive, even when your phone isn't immediately accessible. The watch ensures that every alert feels relevant and actionable, helping you stay on top of communication and updates effortlessly.

1. Receiving Notifications:

The Pixel Watch 3 displays notifications for calls, texts, emails, and apps in real-time.

All notifications that appear on your paired phone will show up on your watch, offering a quick way to stay informed without disrupting your workflow.

Unlike some other devices, notifications on the Pixel Watch 3 appear as standalone messages instead of being bundled together. This makes it easier to read each notification without scrolling through grouped items.

2. Interacting with Notifications:

The Pixel Watch 3 doesn't just display notifications it also allows you to interact with them directly. For instance:

Respond to Messages:

Use preset quick replies or the watch's built-in voice-to-text feature to reply to texts or emails.

Answer or Decline Calls:

Incoming calls can be accepted or rejected with a simple tap, and you can use the watch's built-in speaker and microphone for phone calls when connected via Bluetooth or LTE.

Manage App Alerts:

Customize which app notifications you want to receive on the watch through the Pixel Watch app on your smartphone.

Notifications can be cleared individually, or you can dismiss them all with a single swipe. Clearing a notification on the watch also clears it from your phone, keeping both devices in sync.

3. Customization and Do Not Disturb:

The Pixel Watch 3 allows you to fine-tune how and when you receive notifications:

Priority Notifications:

Choose which apps or contacts can send you alerts while filtering out less critical notifications.

Do Not Disturb Mode:

Activate this mode during meetings, workouts, or sleep to silence notifications and avoid distractions.

Vibration Patterns:

Customize vibration intensity or patterns to differentiate between notification types.

4. Notification Privacy:

To protect your privacy, notifications can be set to display only after you tap the screen or unlock the watch. This feature ensures that sensitive information, like message previews or email details, doesn't appear when the watch is idle.

Connectivity:

The Pixel Watch 3's connectivity features go beyond traditional smartwatch capabilities. With options like Bluetooth, Wi-Fi 6, LTE, NFC, and UWB, the watch is equipped to handle everything from seamless phone syncing to making independent calls and payments.

1. Bluetooth Connectivity:

Bluetooth is the primary method of syncing the Pixel Watch 3 with your smartphone. Ensure Bluetooth is enabled on your phone to pair it with the watch using the Pixel Watch app.

Once paired, Bluetooth ensures that notifications, music playback controls, and health data sync seamlessly between the watch and phone.

The watch uses Bluetooth Low Energy (BLE) technology, which optimizes battery consumption without compromising performance.

2. Wi-Fi 6:

The Pixel Watch 3 supports Wi-Fi 6, providing fast and reliable connectivity even when your phone isn't nearby. Wi-Fi ensures that the watch can:

Download app updates directly.

Receive notifications and alerts when connected to a trusted Wi-Fi network.

To connect to Wi-Fi, navigate to Settings > Connectivity > Wi-Fi on the watch. The device will automatically remember and reconnect to saved networks.

3. LTE (Optional):

If you own the LTE-enabled model of the Pixel Watch 3, you can enjoy full functionality without needing your phone nearby. With LTE, you can:

Make and receive calls directly from the watch.

Send texts or access data-heavy apps like maps and streaming services.

Use apps and services independently of your phone, making the watch an ideal companion for workouts or travel.

Setting up LTE requires a compatible data plan with your carrier. Once activated, you can toggle LTE on or off through the watch's connectivity settings to optimize battery life.

4. NFC for Google Pay:

The Pixel Watch 3 includes NFC (Near Field Communication) technology, enabling contactless payments via Google Pay. Paying with your watch is as simple as holding it near a compatible payment terminal.

To set up Google Pay on the watch:

Open the Pixel Watch app on your phone.

Navigate to the Google Pay section and add your preferred payment method.

Once added, you can double-press the flat button on the watch to activate Google Pay during transactions.

This feature eliminates the need to carry a wallet or phone, making it especially convenient during workouts, commutes, or errands.

5. UWB (Ultra-Wideband):

The Pixel Watch 3's Ultra-Wideband (UWB) technology adds a layer of advanced connectivity for specific use cases, such as:

Seamless Unlocking:

UWB works with compatible Pixel phones to unlock them automatically when the watch is nearby.

Enhanced Smart Home Control:

Future updates will expand UWB functionality to interact with smart home devices more efficiently.

File Sharing:

Transfer files or media between UWB-enabled devices with greater speed and precision compared to Bluetooth.

Practical Use Cases:

The combination of robust notification handling and advanced connectivity makes the Pixel Watch 3 a versatile companion for everyday life. Here are some practical scenarios where these features shine:

1. During Workouts:

Leave your phone behind and rely on LTE or Wi-Fi to stream music, track fitness data, or receive urgent notifications.

Use Bluetooth headphones to listen to music or take calls hands-free.

2. At Work:

Manage notifications discreetly with quick glances, reducing the need to check your phone.

Use Google Pay for quick lunches without pulling out your wallet.

3. While Traveling:

Stay connected in areas with public Wi-Fi or use LTE for navigation and communication.

Make payments with NFC and access maps and translation apps directly on the watch.

4. Smart Home Integration:

Use UWB to interact with compatible devices, such as unlocking doors or transferring files with minimal effort.

The Pixel Watch 3 excels at keeping you connected and informed with its seamless notification system and cutting-edge connectivity options. Whether you're catching up on messages, making contactless payments, or enjoying LTE freedom, this watch ensures that staying connected has never been more convenient. With customizable settings and advanced features, the Pixel Watch 3 adapts to your needs, offering an experience that's not only functional but also intuitive and reliable.

Chapter 6. Managing Apps and Features Downloading Apps:

The Google Pixel Watch 3 provides a rich ecosystem of apps and features, allowing users to customize their experience to fit personal needs. From health and fitness tracking to music and media playback, the watch is designed to be your all-in-one companion. In this chapter, we'll explore how to manage apps effectively and make the most of its features.

Downloading Apps:

Adding apps to your Pixel Watch 3 is a straightforward process, giving you access to countless tools and features tailored for Wear OS. These apps enhance your watch's functionality, whether you're tracking fitness goals, managing productivity, or enjoying entertainment.

1. Accessing the Google Play Store:

The Pixel Watch 3 is equipped with its own Google Play Store app, allowing you to browse and download apps directly to your watch.

Alternatively, you can manage apps through the Pixel Watch app on your smartphone. This provides a more extensive browsing experience on a larger screen.

2. Steps to Download Apps:

On the Watch:

Press the rotating crown to access the app list and tap the Google Play Store icon.

Use the search bar or browse the categories to find apps compatible with Wear OS.

Select the app you want and tap Install. The app will download and appear in your app list.

On Your Phone:

Open the Pixel Watch app and navigate to the Apps section.

Browse for apps in the integrated Play Store or use the search function to find specific ones.

Select the app and choose Install on Watch to push it to your Pixel Watch.

3. Popular App Categories:

Health & Fitness:

Apps like Strava, Nike Run Club, and Calm.

Productivity:

Google Keep for notes, Todoist for task management.

Entertainment:

Spotify, YouTube Music, and Pocket Casts for media streaming.

Utilities:

Weather, stopwatch, and translation apps enhance daily convenience.

4. Managing Apps:

To uninstall apps, navigate to Settings > Apps > Manage Apps on the watch or use the Pixel Watch app on your phone.

Ensure apps are updated regularly by enabling Auto-update in the Play Store settings.

Health and Fitness Apps:

Health and fitness are central to the Pixel Watch 3's appeal. Whether you're an athlete or just trying to stay active, the watch offers robust tracking and analysis tools through Fitbit integration and third-party apps.

1. Fitbit for Comprehensive Health Tracking:

Fitbit, now integrated directly into the Pixel Watch, provides in-depth tracking of workouts, heart rate, sleep, and stress management.

The Fitbit app on your phone syncs seamlessly with the watch to deliver detailed metrics and trends, such as:

Daily Readiness Score:

Evaluates your recovery and readiness for exercise.

Stress Management Score:

Tracks physical stress levels using continuous heart rate and skin conductance sensors.

Set personalized goals for steps, calories, or exercise minutes and monitor your progress directly from the watch.

2. Third-Party Fitness Apps:

Apps like Strava and Nike Run Club are perfect for enthusiasts who prefer advanced features tailored for running, cycling, or other activities.

Specialized apps like Yoga Studio or Seven provide guided workouts directly on your wrist.

3. Activity-Specific Features:

For runners, the Pixel Watch offers metrics like pace, distance, and splits.

Swimmers can track laps and strokes thanks to its IP68 water resistance.

Automatic workout detection logs activities like walking or running, ensuring you never miss a session.

Google Assistant:

The Pixel Watch 3 comes with Google Assistant, making it a versatile device for voice control and smart home management. With just your voice, you can perform tasks or access information hands-free.

1. Activating Google Assistant:

To activate, press and hold the flat button below the rotating crown, or simply say, "Hey Google," if voice activation is enabled.

Follow the setup prompts in the Pixel Watch app to link your Assistant to your Google account.

2. Use Cases:

Reminders and Alarms:

"Set a reminder for my meeting at 2 PM," or "Wake me up at 7 AM."

Smart Home Control:

Adjust lights, thermostats, or check your security cameras with voice commands. For example, "Turn off the living room lights."

Quick Information:

Ask questions like, "What's the weather today?" or "How many calories are in an apple?"

Navigational Help:

Get step-by-step directions or find nearby restaurants while on the go.

3. Integration with Other Features:

Combine Assistant with other apps for seamless workflows. For instance, you can ask it to play music, send a text, or start a workout.

Music and Media:

The Pixel Watch 3 makes entertainment accessible no matter where you are, offering integration with popular music and media apps.

1. Streaming Services:

Spotify: Stream your favorite playlists or podcasts directly from the watch when connected to Wi-Fi or LTE.

YouTube Music:

Enjoy on-demand music and download tracks for offline listening. Premium users can sync playlists to the watch for phone-free playback.

Other apps like Pocket Casts ensure your podcasts are always within reach.

2. Music Playback:

Control music on your phone from the watch:

Adjust volume, skip tracks, or pause/play directly from the watch's interface.

Use the rotating crown for precise volume control.

Pair Bluetooth headphones with the watch for a fully mobile listening experience. Go to Settings > Connectivity > Bluetooth to connect your headphones.

3. Offline Media:

For offline use, download music or podcasts to the watch via apps like YouTube Music or Spotify.

Once downloaded, media can be played directly from the watch without needing a phone connection, ideal for workouts or commutes.

4. Media Controls:

Media controls appear as notifications when playing music or videos on your paired phone. These allow you to manage playback without opening apps.

Practical Tips for Maximizing Apps and Features

1. Keep Apps Organized:

Use the Pixel Watch app on your phone to rearrange app shortcuts on your watch for quicker access.

Frequently used apps can be assigned to the flat button's shortcut menu.

2. Battery Optimization:

Limit background activity for apps that consume excessive power.

Use the Battery Saver Mode to extend usage during long days.

3. Leverage Ecosystem Integration:

The Pixel Watch works seamlessly with Google services like Gmail, Calendar, and Maps. Ensure these apps are installed and synced for a unified experience.

4. Experiment with New Apps:

Regularly explore the Google Play Store for new apps that enhance your watch's functionality. Many developers release updates and new tools tailored for Wear OS.

The Pixel Watch 3 transforms how you manage apps and features, offering unparalleled flexibility and ease of use. Whether you're tracking your fitness journey, enjoying music on the go, or staying organized with Google Assistant, the watch ensures that everything you need is just a tap—or voice command—away. By understanding how to download, customize, and optimize apps, you can tailor your watch to fit your lifestyle perfectly.

Chapter 7.

Battery and Charging

Battery performance is a critical factor in the user experience of any smartwatch, and the Google Pixel Watch 3 offers robust battery life and efficient charging capabilities. With thoughtful usage and management, the watch ensures you stay connected and powered throughout your day. This chapter explores battery life, power-saving strategies, and best practices for charging your device.

Battery Life Overview:

The battery life of the Pixel Watch 3 varies depending on the model and usage patterns.

1. Standard Battery Life:

41mm Model:

This version is optimized for smaller wrists and provides up to 24 hours of battery life on a full charge.

45mm Model:

Equipped with a larger battery, this model offers up to 36 hours, making it ideal for users who require longer usage without frequent charging.

2. Factors Influencing Battery Life:

Display Usage:

The always-on display (AOD) consumes more power, particularly in bright environments. Turning off AOD or lowering screen brightness can significantly extend battery life.

Sensors and Tracking:

Features like continuous heart rate monitoring, GPS, and SpO2 tracking are beneficial but consume considerable power.

Connectivity:

Using Wi-Fi, Bluetooth, LTE (if available), or streaming music also impacts battery performance.

Apps and Notifications:

Running multiple apps in the background or receiving frequent notifications can deplete the battery faster.

3. Real-World Scenarios:

Moderate use of notifications, fitness tracking, and music playback can provide a full day of use on the 41mm model and nearly two days on the 45mm model.

Heavy usage, such as prolonged GPS tracking or streaming, may reduce these estimates.

Battery Saver Mode:

Battery Saver Mode is an essential feature that helps extend the watch's battery life when you're running low on power.

1. How It Works:

Battery Saver Mode disables non-essential features like always-on display, continuous health monitoring, and background app activity.

Basic functionality like the watch face and notifications remain active, ensuring you don't miss critical updates.

2. Activating Battery Saver Mode:

Swipe down on the watch face to access the Quick Settings menu.

Tap the Battery Saver icon to enable or disable the feature as needed.

Alternatively, navigate to Settings > Battery > Battery Saver to activate it manually.

3. When to Use It:

Activate Battery Saver Mode during extended periods without access to a charger, such as travel or outdoor adventures.

Enable it preemptively if the battery level drops below 20% and you need the watch to last several more hours.

4. Customization Options:

You can customize Battery Saver Mode settings to keep certain features active, such as notifications or step tracking, while limiting others.

Charging Your Pixel Watch 3:

Charging your Pixel Watch 3 is simple and efficient. It uses a magnetic charging dock, which ensures the device aligns correctly and charges securely.

1. Charging Process:

Connect the magnetic charging dock to a USB-C power adapter or USB port.

Place the watch face-up on the dock, ensuring the back aligns with the magnetic contacts. A charging indicator will appear on the screen.

The watch typically takes 1-2 hours to reach a full charge.

2. Fast Charging:

The Pixel Watch 3 supports fast charging, allowing you to quickly top up the battery when needed. For example:

A 15-minute charge can provide enough power for several hours of basic use.

A 30-minute charge often restores the battery to 50% or more, depending on the model.

3. Charging Tips:

Avoid using third-party chargers not certified for the Pixel Watch 3 to prevent damage to the battery.

Charge the watch in a well-ventilated area to prevent overheating.

Use a high-quality power adapter to maximize charging efficiency.

Best Practices for Prolonging Battery Life:

Taking care of your Pixel Watch 3's battery ensures long-term performance and reliability.

1. Optimize Display Settings:

Reduce screen brightness manually or enable Auto-Brightness to adjust according to lighting conditions.

Turn off the always-on display if you don't need the time visible constantly.

2. Manage Health Tracking:

Use continuous heart rate and SpO2 tracking selectively, such as during workouts or sleep monitoring.

Disable background tracking features like skin temperature monitoring when not needed.

3. Control Connectivity:

Turn off Wi-Fi or LTE when you're not actively using them, as these features drain battery power.

Enable Airplane Mode in situations where connectivity is unnecessary, such as during flights or long meetings.

4. Limit Notifications:

Customize which notifications you receive on the watch by adjusting settings in the Pixel Watch app. Receiving only critical notifications reduces battery drain.

5. Close Background Apps:

Regularly check and close apps running in the background to conserve power.

6. Use Battery Saver Mode:

Enable it preemptively when you know you'll have limited access to charging facilities.

Troubleshooting Battery Issues:

If you notice unusual battery performance, follow these steps to diagnose and resolve the issue:

1. Check Battery Usage:

Navigate to Settings > Battery > Battery Usage to view which apps or features are consuming the most power.

2. Update Software:

Ensure your Pixel Watch 3 is running the latest firmware, as updates often include battery optimization fixes.

3. Restart the Watch:

Restarting the device can resolve temporary glitches that may cause rapid battery drain.

4. Reset to Factory Settings:

If battery issues persist, consider performing a factory reset via Settings > System > Reset. Be sure to back up your data first.

A Day in the Life:

Practical Battery Usage Scenarios

1. Active Workday (41mm Model):

Morning:

Enable notifications and track your commute with Google Maps (10% usage).

Midday:

Track a 30-minute workout with heart rate monitoring (15% usage).

Evening:

Stream music via Bluetooth while cooking (10% usage).

Battery Remaining:

Approximately 65% after moderate use.

2. Outdoor Adventure (45mm Model):

Morning: Use GPS for a 2-hour hike (25% usage).

Afternoon:

Take calls and respond to messages with LTE (15% usage).

Evening:

Enable Battery Saver Mode for extended standby time.

Battery Remaining:

25% after a full day of intensive use.

The Pixel Watch 3 strikes a balance between performance and power efficiency. By understanding its battery capabilities and implementing smart charging and power-saving habits, you can maximize the device's potential and keep it running smoothly throughout your day. Whether you're navigating daily tasks or enjoying outdoor activities, the watch ensures that power is one less thing to worry about.

Chapter 8.
Troubleshooting and Maintenance Software Updates:

Owning a Pixel Watch 3 brings a premium smartwatch experience, but like any sophisticated device, it requires proper care and occasional troubleshooting to maintain peak performance. This chapter explores essential maintenance tips, how to handle software updates, and practical solutions for common issues. Additionally, we discuss the watch's fragility and ways to protect it from damage.

Software Updates:

Software updates are critical for keeping your Pixel Watch 3 running smoothly and securely. Updates deliver new features, bug fixes, and security patches, ensuring your device stays up-to-date with the latest Wear OS improvements.

1. Why Regular Updates Matter:

Performance Enhancements:

Updates can improve speed, battery life, and overall functionality.

Bug Fixes:

Known issues, such as app crashes or connectivity problems, are often resolved through updates.

New Features:

Google regularly adds new capabilities to Wear OS, such as expanded app support or enhanced health tracking.

Security Patches:

Updates protect your watch from vulnerabilities, keeping your data safe.

2. How to Update Your Pixel Watch 3:

Ensure your watch is connected to Wi-Fi and has at least 50% battery charge or is placed on its charger.

Open the Settings app on your watch.

Navigate to System > Software Update. The watch will automatically check for updates.

If an update is available, follow the on-screen instructions to download and install it. The process typically takes a few minutes, depending on the update size.

3. Using the Pixel Watch App:

The Pixel Watch app on your phone will notify you of available updates.

Open the app, go to Watch Settings, and tap System Updates to initiate the process.

4. Tips for Smooth Updates:

Avoid interrupting the update process, as this may cause issues.

If the update fails, restart your watch and try again.

Ensure both your phone and watch have a stable internet connection during the update.

Resetting the Watch:

Occasionally, you might encounter issues that require resetting your Pixel Watch 3. Resetting is a last resort but can effectively resolve persistent problems.

1. When to Reset:

The watch becomes unresponsive or freezes frequently.

Apps fail to launch, or system features malfunction.

You plan to sell or gift the watch and need to erase personal data.

2. Types of Resets:

Soft Reset:

Restart your watch by holding down the crown button until the screen turns off and the Google logo appears. This method resolves minor glitches without erasing data.

Factory Reset:

A more comprehensive reset that erases all data and restores the watch to its original settings.

3. Steps for a Factory Reset:

On your watch, open Settings.

Navigate to System > Reset Options > Erase All Data.

Confirm the action. The watch will reboot and wipe all data.

4. Important Considerations:

Back Up Data:

Before resetting, ensure your health data, app settings, and watch faces are synced to your Google account or Fitbit account.

Re-pairing the Watch: After resetting, you will need to pair the watch with your phone again and reconfigure settings.

Handling Fragility:

The Pixel Watch 3 features a stunning, curved glass dome that enhances its sleek design. However, its delicate construction requires special care to prevent scratches or cracks.

1. Protecting the Watch:

Screen Protectors:

Invest in a high-quality tempered glass or film protector to shield the display from scratches and minor impacts.

Protective Cases:

Slim cases designed for the Pixel Watch 3 add a layer of protection without compromising aesthetics.

Careful Usage:

Avoid exposing the watch to harsh environments, such as construction sites or areas with loose debris.

2. Common Scenarios of Damage:

Dropping the watch onto hard surfaces can shatter the glass.

Accidental scrapes against metal edges or abrasive surfaces can cause scratches.

Wearing the watch during high-contact sports without a case increases the risk of damage.

3. What to Do If Damaged:

Unfortunately, the Pixel Watch 3 does not support repair services for its glass dome or internal components.

If the watch sustains significant damage, your only option is to replace it entirely. Consider purchasing device protection plans or warranties when buying the watch.

Troubleshooting Common Issues:

While the Pixel Watch 3 is a high-performance device, occasional issues may arise. Here's how to handle some common problems:

1. Connectivity Problems:

Issue: The watch won't sync with your phone.

Solution:

Restart both the watch and phone.

Ensure Bluetooth is enabled on both devices.

Re-pair the devices through the Pixel Watch app.

2. Battery Drains Quickly:

Issue:

The watch isn't lasting as long as expected.

Solution:

Check Battery Usage in settings to identify power-hungry apps.

Disable unnecessary features like always-on display or GPS when not in use.

Activate Battery Saver Mode for extended life.

3. Unresponsive Screen:

Issue:

The watch's touchscreen doesn't respond.

Solution:

Perform a soft reset by holding down the crown button until the watch restarts.

Ensure the screen is clean and free of water or debris.

4. App Crashes or Freezes:

Issue:

Apps fail to load or crash frequently.

Solution:

Update the apps through the Google Play Store.

Uninstall and reinstall problematic apps.

5. Overheating:

Issue:

The watch feels excessively warm.

Solution:

Remove it from your wrist and allow it to cool down.

Avoid charging the watch in hot environments.

Limit power-intensive features, such as LTE or GPS, during extended use.

Long-Term Maintenance Tips:

1. Clean the Watch Regularly:

Use a soft, damp cloth to wipe the display and sensors.

Avoid using abrasive cleaners or alcohol-based solutions that may damage the finish.

2. Store Properly:

When not in use, store the watch in a cool, dry place.

Avoid prolonged exposure to direct sunlight or extreme temperatures.

3. Check Straps and Accessories:

Periodically inspect the watch straps for wear and tear.

Replace straps as needed to maintain comfort and security.

4. Keep Software Updated:

Regular updates not only enhance features but also address potential bugs that could impact performance.

By following these tips, you can ensure your Pixel Watch 3 remains a reliable and stylish companion for years to come. Proper maintenance and swift troubleshooting allow you to make the most of this premium wearable device.

Chapter 9.

Additional Features and Tips Wear OS Features:

The Google Pixel Watch 3 offers a suite of features that extend beyond basic fitness tracking and notifications. Powered by Wear OS, it integrates seamlessly with Google services and third-party apps, providing an all-in-one experience for productivity, fitness, and convenience. This chapter delves into the standout features, practical tips for maximizing their use, and insights into enhancing your overall experience.

Wear OS Features:

Wear OS is the heart of the Pixel Watch 3, delivering a polished and intuitive interface. Here are some of the standout features available:

Google Pay for Contactless Payments:

Google Pay transforms your Pixel Watch into a convenient, wrist-based wallet for contactless payments.

1. Setting Up Google Pay:

Open the Pixel Watch app on your phone.

Navigate to Payments & Wallet, and follow the steps to add your credit or debit card.

Ensure your card issuer supports Google Pay for Wear OS.

2. Making Payments:

Double-press the flat button beneath the crown to launch Google Pay.

Hold your watch close to the payment terminal until the transaction is confirmed.

A vibration or sound indicates the payment was successful.

3. Tips for Secure Transactions:

Use a strong PIN or password to secure your watch.

Enable Find My Device in case your watch is misplaced or stolen.

Regularly review transaction history through the Google Pay app on your phone.

Google Assistant for Voice Control:

Google Assistant serves as your personal AI companion, making it easier to interact with your watch hands-free.

1. Activating Google Assistant:

Press and hold the flat button or say, "Hey Google," if voice activation is enabled.

Customize settings in the Pixel Watch app under Assistant Settings.

2. What You Can Do:

Set Reminders:

"Remind me to take my medication at 8 PM."

Control Smart Home Devices:

Adjust lights, thermostats, or security cameras through the Google Home app.

Check Weather:

"What's the weather like tomorrow?"

Manage Tasks:

Add items to your Google Keep or to-do lists.

Navigate:

Ask for directions, and Google Maps will provide turn-by-turn guidance.

3. Pro Tips:

Use shortcuts for repetitive tasks (e.g., "Start my morning routine").

Enable Personalized Results in Assistant settings for tailored responses.

Fitness Challenges via the Fitbit App:

The integration of Fitbit on the Pixel Watch 3 makes fitness tracking more engaging and interactive through challenges.

1. Setting Up Challenges:

Open the Fitbit app on your phone and go to the Challenges & Adventures section.

Select from available options, such as step goals, distance challenges, or virtual trails.

Invite friends to participate for added motivation.

2. Benefits of Challenges:

Keeps you accountable for your fitness goals.

Adds a competitive edge with leaderboards and achievement badges.

Syncs seamlessly with your watch, providing real-time updates.

3. Tips for Success:

Set realistic goals that match your fitness level.

Use the watch's Active Zone Minutes feature to measure workout intensity.

Reward yourself for milestones to maintain motivation.

Access Smart Home Devices with Google Home:

Control your smart home ecosystem directly from your Pixel Watch using the Google Home app.

1. Setting Up Smart Devices:

Download the Google Home app on your phone and link compatible smart devices.

Sync the app to your Pixel Watch for easy access.

2. How to Use Smart Home Controls:

Open the Google Home app on your watch.

View and manage devices such as lights, speakers, cameras, and thermostats.

Use Google Assistant commands for voice control (e.g., "Turn off the living room lights").

3. Practical Applications:

Morning Routines:

Set up routines to adjust your lights, coffee maker, and thermostat with a single tap.

Security Monitoring:

Check live feeds from connected security cameras directly on your watch.

Energy Management:

Turn off appliances or adjust thermostat settings when away from home.

4. Tips for Smart Home Integration:

Organize devices into groups (e.g., "Living Room" or "Bedroom") for easier management.

Enable notifications for critical alerts, such as motion detection or doorbell rings.

Use schedules and automation to reduce manual control.

Additional Tips for Maximizing Pixel Watch 3 Features:

1. Customizing Wear OS:

Download third-party apps from the Google Play Store to expand functionality, such as language translators, meditation guides, or travel planners.

Personalize watch faces to display useful information, like daily agenda, weather, or step count.

2. Optimizing Battery Life:

Use Battery Saver Mode during periods of low activity.

Disable always-on display or reduce brightness when not needed.

Close background apps that are not in use.

3. Enhancing Productivity:

Sync your calendar and email accounts for on-wrist notifications.

Use Google Keep to view and manage shopping or task lists directly on the watch.

Set alarms and timers for time-sensitive activities.

4. Exploring Offline Features:

Download music from Spotify or YouTube Music for offline playback during workouts.

Save maps offline with Google Maps for navigation without an active connection.

Preload your favorite apps for uninterrupted use during travel.

5. Regular Maintenance:

Keep the watch software updated for new features and security patches.

Clean the watch regularly to maintain sensors' accuracy and aesthetics.

Inspect straps for wear and replace them as necessary.

Conclusion:

The Pixel Watch 3, powered by Wear OS, offers a versatile range of features designed to enhance every aspect of your daily life. From seamless payment options and voice control to fitness challenges and smart home management, the watch serves as an indispensable companion for modern living. By exploring these capabilities and implementing the tips provided, you can unlock the full potential of your Pixel Watch 3 while tailoring it to your unique lifestyle.